BST BEST NOTES

SHARP YOUR MIND

I0483026

MJ BROS.

XpressPublishing
An imprint of Notion Press

Old No. 38, New No. 6
McNichols Road, Chetpet
Chennai - 600 031

First Published by Notion Press 2019
Copyright © MJ Bros. 2019
All Rights Reserved.

ISBN 978-1-64661-531-5

Contents

1

1. Management is defined as the process of planning, organising and controlling an organisation's operations in order to achieve the target efficiently and effectively. It is essential for all organisations.

2. Concepts of Management

Traditional Concept Management is the art of getting things done through others.

Modern Concept Management is defined as the process (refers to the basic steps) to get the things done with the aim of achieving goals effectively and efficiently (effectiveness refers to achievement of task on time and efficiently implies optimum use of resources).

3. Characteristics of Management

(i) Management is a Goal Oriented Process Organisation'S existence is based on objectives and management is the process which unites the efforts of
every individuals to achieve the goal.

(ii) Management is All Pervasive The use of management is not restricted, it is applicable in all organisations big or small, profit or non-profit making.

(iii) Management is Multidimensional it does not contain one activity. it is a complex activity including three main activities

(a) Management of house
(b) Management of people
(c) Management of operations

(iv) Management is a Continuous Process It is a never ending process. It consists of series of interrelated functions which performs continuously.

(v) Management is a Group Activity Organisation is a collection of many individuals, every individual contributes towards achieving the goal.

(vi) Management is an Intangible Force It cannot be seen or touched only it can be felt in the way the organisation functions.

4. Objectives of Management Objectives can be classified into organisational. social or personal

(i) Organisational Objectives

(a) Survival It exists for a long time in the competition market.

(b) Profit It provides a vital incentive for the continued successful operations.

(c) Growth Success of an organisation is measured by growth and expansion of activities.

(ii) Social Objectives Involves creation of benefit for society.

(iii) Personal Objectives Objectives of employees like good salary, promotion, social recognition, healthy working conditions.

5. Importance of Management

(i) Management Helps Achieving Group Goals It integrates the objective of individual along with organisational goal.

(ii) Management Increases Efficiency It increases productivity through better planning, organising, directing the activities of the organisation.

(iii) Management Creates a Dynamic Organisation Organisation have to survive in dynamic environment thus manager keep changes in the organisation to match environmental changes.

(iv) ManagementHelps in Achieving Personal Objectives Through motivation and leadership, management helps in achieving the personal objectives.

(v) Management Helps in the Development of Society It provides good quality products and services. creates employment. generate new technology in that sense it helps in the development of the society.

6. Management as an Art Management as an art because it satisfies following points

It is based on practice and creativity.

Lots of literature is present which gives the existence of theoretical knowledge.

7. Management as a Science Management as a science because

It is a systematised body of knowledge.

Its principles are based on experimentation.

8. Management as a Profession It docs not meet the exact criterion of a profession. it does have some features of a profession.

9. Levels of Management

Top Management It consists of senior most executives who are usually referred to as the Chairman, Chief Executive Officer, President and Vice

President.

Middle Management They are usually division heads who are the link between top and lower level of management.

Operational Management They are usually the foremen and supervisors who actually carryon the work or perform the activities.

10. Functions of Management

Planning It refers to deciding in advance what to do, how to do and developing a may of achieving goal efficiently and effectively.

Organising It refers to the assigning of duties, grouping tasks, establishing authority and allocating of resources required to carry out a specific plan.

Staffing It implies right people for the right. job.

Directing It involves leading, mfluencing. motivating employees to perform the task assigned to them.

Controlling It refers to the performance measurement and follow up actions that keep the actual performance on the path of plan.

11. Co-ordination-The Essence of Management Co-ordination means binding together all the activities such as purchase, production. saJes. finance to ensure continuity in the working of the organisation. It is considered as a separate function of management, in order to achieve harmony among individual. efforts towards the accomplishment of goods.

12. Characteristics of Co-ordination

It integrates group efforts.

It ensures units of action.

It is a continuous process.

It is an all pervasive function.

It is the responsibility of all managers.

13. Importance of Co-ordination

Growth in Size When there is a growth in size, the number of people employed by the organisation also increases. Thus to integrate the efforts. co-ordination is needed.

Functional Differentiation In an organisation. there are separate department and different goals. The process of linking those activities is achieved by co-ordination.

Specialisation Modern organisation is characterised by a high degree of specialisation. Co-ordination is required among different specialists because of their different approaches, judgement etc.

2

Principle It refers to a statement which reflects the fundamental truth about some phenomenon based on cause and effect relationship.

2. Management Principles These are the statements of fundamental truth, they serve as a guide to thought and actions for managerial decision actions and their execution.

3. Derivation of Management Principles

Management principles have been derived on the basis of

(i) Deep observations

(ii) Repeated experiments

4. Nature of Principles of Management

(i) Universal Applicability The principles of management are universal in nature that means they can be applied to all types of organisations irrespective of their size and nature.

(ii) General Guidelines Management principle give guidelines to solve the problems, these principles do not provide ready made solution for all the problems.

(iii) Formed by Practice and Experiments The management principles are developed only after deep and through research work.

(iv) Flexibility These are not set of rigid statements. These can be modified by the managers who are using them.

(v) Mainly Behavioural Management principles are formed to guide and influence the behaviour of employees.

(vi) Cause and Effect Relationship Management principles are based on cause and effect that means these principles tell us if a particular principle is applied in a situation, what might be the effect.

(vii) Contingent Management principles are contingent or dependent upon the situation prevailing in organisation.

5. Significance of Principles of Management

(i) Providing managers with useful insight into reality

(ii) Optimum utilisation of the resources

(iii) Scientific decisions

(iv) Meeting changing environment requirements

(v) Fulfilling social responsibility

(vi) Management training, education and research

6. Background and History of Henry Fayol

Henry Fayol was born in France in 1841. He got degree in mining engineering in 1860 and started working as engineer in a Coal Mining Company. In 1888. be was promoted as the Managing Director of the company. At that time. the company was in the situation of insolvency. He accepted the challenge and applied his managerial techniques to bring out the company from this situation and he succeeded. When he retired after 30 years, the company was a leading coal-steel company with strong financial background.

7. Principles of Management Developed by Henry Fayol

(i) Principle of division of work

(ii) Principle of authority and responsibility

(iii) Principle of discipline

(iv) Principle of unity of command

(v) Unity of direction

(vi) Subordination of individual interest to general interest

(vii) Remuneration of employees

(viii) Centralisation and decentralisation

(ix) Scalar chain

(x) Order

(xi) Equity

(xii) Stability of personal

(xiii) Initiative

(xiv) Esprit de Corps

8. Scientific Management It can be defined as "Application science for each and every element of management."

According to Taylor, "Scientific management means knowing exactly what you want men to do and seeing that they do it in the best and cheapest way."

9. Scientific Principles of Management

(i) Science, not rule of thumb

(ii) Harmony, not discord

(iii) Co-operation, not individualism

(iv) Development of workers to their prosperity greatest efficiency and

10. Scientific Techniques of Taylor

(i) Functional Foremanship In this technique, Taylor suggested the division of factory in two departments

(a) Planning Department

Route clerk

Instruction card clerk

Time and cost clerk

Disciplinarian

(b) Operational Department

Gang boss

Speed boss

Repair boss

Inspector

(ii) Standardisation and Simplification of Work

Standardisation output possible if standard is maintained right from selection of tools, equipment and machine to use.

Simplification emphasises on elimination of unnecessary diversity of product, size and type.

(iii) Fatigue Study This technique of scientific management is conducted to find out

(a) The frequency of rest intervals

(b) The duration of rest intervals

(c) The number of rest intervals

(iv) Method Study This technique find out the one best method or way of performing the job.

(v) Time Study The objectives of time study are

(a) The standard time required to perform a job.

(b) Setting up the standard target of the workers.

(c) Determining the number of workers required to perform a job.

(d) Categorising the workers into efficient and inefficient employees.

(vi) Motion Study To conduct motion study, Taylor suggested to observe an average worker when he is performing the job and note down all the movements he is doing.

(vii) Differential Piece Wage System This technique emphasis on paying different rate of wage for efficient and inefficient employees.

(viii) Mental Revolution 'The objectives of mental revolution are

(a) Co-operation between workers and management.

(b) Change in mental attitudes of workers and management towards each other.

3

1. Business Environment Business environment as such is the total of all external forces which affect the organisation and operation of business.

2. Features/Characteristics of Business Environment

Totality of External Force Business environment includes all the external forces so it is aggregative in nature.

Specific and General Forces Business environment includes both specific and general forces. Specific forces such as investors. customers affect business directly.General forces auch as social. political. legal and technological conditions.

Inter-relatednes All the forces and factors of business are inter-related.

Dynamic Nature Business environment is dynamic in nature. It keeps on changing whether in terms of technological unprovements.

Uncertainty Business environment is uncertain and these changes are difficult to predict

Complexity BusIness environment is difficult to understand. It can be understood easily in parts but in totality it is difficult to understand.

3. Importance of Business Environment

Environment Provides Numerous Opportunities for Business Success It enables the firm to identify opportunities and getting the first mover advantage.

Threats and Early Warning Signals Environmental awareness can help managers to identify various threats on time and serve as an early warning signal.

It Helps in Tapping Useful Resources Environment is a source of various resources for running a business. Like as finance, machines, raw materials etc.

It Helps in Copying with Rapid Changes Knowledge of environmental changes sensitises the management to make new strategy to copy with the emerging problems of changes.

It Helps in Assisting in Planning and Policy Formulation Its understanding and analysis can be the basis for deciding the future course of action or training guidelines for decision making.

It helps in Improving Performance With continuous scan of business environment, companies can easily improve their performance.

4. Dimensions of Business Environment

Economic Environment It consists of Gross Domestic product, Income at National level and per capital level. Profit earning rate, monetary and fiscal policy of the government etc.

Social Environment It consists of the customs and traditions of the society in which business is existing. It includes the standard of living. taste, preferences etc.

Political Environment It constitutes all the factors related to government affairs such as type of government, power, attitude of government towards different groups of societies etc.

Legal Environment It constitutes the laws and various legislations passed in the parliament. Like as Trade Mark Act, Essential Commodity Act, Weights and Measures Act etc.

Technological Environment It refers to changes taking place in the method of production, use of equipments and machineries to improves the quality of product.

5. Economic Environment in India

Since 1991 India has been going on economic reforms. We have now adopted the policy of liberalisation, privatisation and globalisation, We have started modernising the country's industrial system.Unproductive control are being removed private investment, including foreign investment is being encouraged.

(i) Liberalisation It means removing unnecessary trade restrictions and making the economy more competitive like as freedom of production, expansion of industries.

(ii) Privatisation It means removing strict control over private sector and making them free to take necessary decisions. Like as reduction in the number of reserved public sector industries, increasing the share of private sector investment.

(iii) Globalisation Free interaction among economies of the world in the field of trade, finance, production, technologies and investment is termed as globalisation. Our new economic policy contributed towards globalisation in the following ways.

(a) Devaluation of rupee

(b) Raising foreign equity participation

(c) Long period trade policy

(d) Convertability of rupee

6. Impact of Government Policy Changes on Business and Industry

Increasing Competition There is a tough competition between multinationals and there is also competitions between Indian enterprises and foreign enterprises.

More Demanding Customers Customers today become more demanding because they are well-informed.

World Class Technology Changes in government policy regarding business and industry has provided us with world class technology.

Necessity for Change After 1991, the market forces have become turbulent as a result of which the enterprises have to continuously modify their operations.

Need for Developing Human Resource The new market conditions requires people with higher competence and greater commitment.

Market Orientation Today firms are market oriented. They research the market, need and wants of consumers and then they produce good accordingly.

Loss of Budgetary Support to Public Sectors The government's budgetary support for financing the public sector has declined over the years.

1. Planning Planning can be defined as "thinking in advance what. is to be done. when it is to be done, how it is to be done and by whom it should be done."

According to Fayol, "Planning is chalking out plan of action. i.e., the result envisaged in the line of action to be followed. the stages to go through the methods to use."

2. Importance of Planning

(i) Planning Provides Directions Planning provides the directions to the efforts of employees. Planning makes clear what employees have to do. how to do etc.

(ii) Planning Reduces the Risk Uncertainty Planning helps the manager to face the uncertainty because planners try to force the future by making some assumptions. The plans are made to over come uncertainties.

(iii) Planning Reduces Over Lapping and Wasteful Activities Planning evaluates the alternatives uses of the available and prospective resources of the business and makes their must appropriate use.

(iv) Planning Promotes Innovative Ideas Planning requires high thinking and it is an intellectual process. So it makes the managers innovative and creative.

(v) Planning Facilitates Decision Making Planning helps the managers to look in to the future and make a choice from amongst various alternative courses of action.

(vi) Planning Establishes Standards for Controlling It has predetermined goal with which the actual performances are compared to find out deviation and suggest remedial measures.

3. Features of Planning

(i) Planning Focuses on Achieving Objective Planning is purposeful. It has no meaning unless it contributes to the achievement of predetermined organisational goals.

(ii) Planning is a Primary Function of Management PLanning is the primary or first function to be performed by every manager. No other function can be executed by the manager without performing planning function.

(iii) Planning is Pervasive Planning is essential for every sort of business activities. Every department whether, purchase, sales accounts, auditing, marketing etc needs systematic planning.

(iv) Planning is Continuous Planning is a never ending or continuous process because after making plans also one has to be in touch with the changes in changing environment and in the selection of one best way.

(v) Planning is Futuristic Planning always means looking ahead, it is never for the past. All the managers tTY to make predictions and assumptions for future.

(vi) Planning Involves Decision Making Planning choice making of the best possible alternative out of various alternatives.

4. Limitations of Planning

(i) Planning Leads to Rigidity Once plans are made to decide the future course of action the manager may not be in a position to change them.

(ii) Planning May Not Work in a Dynamic Environment

Business environment is very dynamic as there are continuously changes. It becomes very difficult. to forecast these future changes. Plans may fail if the changes are very frequent.

(iii) Planning Reduces Creativity With the planning the managers of the organisation start working rigidly and they become the blind followers of the plan only.

(iv) Planning Involves Huge Costs Planning process involves lot of cost because it is an intellectual process and companies need to hire the professional experts to carry on this process.

(v) Planning is a Time Consuming Success Lot of time is needed in developing planning premises.

(vi) Planning does not Guarantee Success Planning only provides a base for analysing future. It is not a solution for future course of action.

5. Planning Process

(i) Setting Objectives In planning function manager begin with setting up of objectives because all the policies procedures and methods are framed for achieving objectives only.

(ii) Developing Premises Premises refers to making assumptions regarding future. The assumptions are made on the basis of forecasting.

Forecast is the technique of gathering information.

(iii) Identifying Alternative Courses of Action After setting up of objectives the managers make a list of alternatives through which the organisation can achieve its objectives.

(iv) Evaluating Alternative Courses After making the list of various alternatives along with the assumptions supporting them the manager starts evaluating each and every alternative.

(v) Selecting an Alternative The best. alternative is selected but as such there is no mathematical formula to select the best alternative. Some times instead of selecting one alternative a combination of different alternatives can also be selected.

(vi) Implementing the Plan This is the step where other managerial functions also come in to the picture. The step is concerned with putting the plan into action i.e., doing what is required.

(vii) Follow-up Action Planning is a continuous process so the manager's job does not get over simply by putting the plan into action. The manager monitor the plan carefully while it is implemented.

6. Types of Plans

(i) Objectives Objectives are the ends towards which the activities are directed. They axe the end result of every activity. e.g., increase in sale by 10%.

(ii) Strategy A strategy is a comprehensive plan to achieve the organisational objectives.

(iii) Policies Policies are genera] statements that guide thinking or channelise energies towards a particular direction.

(iv) Procedures Procedures are required steps established in advance to handle future conditions. The procedure can be defined as the exact manner in which an activity has to be accomplished.

(v) Method Methods provide the prescribed ways or manner in which a task has to be performed considering the objective.

(vi) Rule Rules are specific statements that inform what is to be done. They do not allow for any flexibility or discretion.

(vii) Programme Programme are detailed statements about a project which outlines the objectives, policies, procedures, rules.

(viii) Budget A budget is a statement of expected results expressed in numerical terms

5

1. Organising Identifying and grouping different activities in the organisation and bringing together the physical, financial and human resources to establish most productive relations for the achievement of specific goal of organisation.

According to Henry Fayol, "To organise a business is to provide it with everything useful to its functioning; raw materials, machines and tools, capital and personnel."

2. Process of Organising
Identification and division of work
Departmentalisation
Assignment of duties
Establishing reporting relationships

3. Importance of Organising
Benefits of specialisation
Clarity in working relationships
Optimum utilisation of resources ·
Adaptation to change
Effective administration
Development of personnel
Expansion and growth

4. Organisation Structure It can be defined as "Network of job positions, responsibilities and authority at different levels."

The considerations to be kept in mind while farming the organisational structure are
Job Design
Departmentation
Span of management
Delegation of authority

5. Types of Organisation Structure The organisational structure can mainly be of two types which are

(i) Functional Structure When the activities or jobs are grouped keeping in mind the functions or the job then it is called functional structure.

(a) Advantages

Specialisation

Easy supervision

Easy co-ordination

It helps in increasing managerial efficiency

Effective training

(b) Disadvantages

Tho departments become specialised ill their own way only.

When departments become too large then the co-ordination decrease.

When the organisational goals is not achieved then it becomes very difficult to make anyone department accountable.

Employees get training of one function only i.e., the department to which they belongs so they can not be shifted to other department.

(c) Suitability It is most suitable when the size of the organisation is large, has diversified activities and operations require a high degree of specialisation.

(ii) Divisional Structure When the organisation is large in size and is producing more than one type of product then activities related to one product are grouped under one department.

(a) Advantages

Product specialisation

Fast decision making

Accountability

Flexibility

Expansion and growth

(b) Disadvantages

Each department will require all the resources as every division will be working as an independent unit.

Conflict on allocation of resources.

Each department focusses on their product only and they fail to keep themselves as a part of one common organisa tion

(c) Suitability

Organisation producing multi product.

Organisation which require product specialisation.

Growing companies which plan to add more line of products in future.

6. Formal Organisation When the managers are carrying on organising process then as a result of organisation process an organisational structure is created to achieve systematic working and efficient utilisation of resources. This type structure is known as formal organisational structure.

(i) Advantages

(a) Systematic working

(b) Achievement of organisational objectives

(c) No overlapping of work

(d) Co-ordination

(e) Creation of chain of command

(f) More emphasis on work

(ii) Disadvantages

(a) Delay in action

(b) Ignores social needs of employees

(c) Emphasis on work only

7. Informal Organisation It is a network of personal and social relations not established or required by the organisation but arising spontaneously as people associate with one another.

(i) Advantages

(a) Fast communication

(b) Fulfills social needs

(c) Correct feedback

(ii) Disadvantages

(a) Spread rumours

(b) No systematic working

(c) May bring negative results

(d) More emphasis to individual interest

8. Delegation of Authority "A process of entrusting responsibility and authority to the subordinates and creating accountability on those employees who are entrusted responsibility and authority."

9. Importance of Delegation

Effective management

Employee development

Motivation of employees

Facilitation of growth

Basis of management hierarchy

Better co-ordination

10. Elements of Delegation

(i) Responsibility It means the work assigned to an individual. It includes all the physical and mental activities to be performed by the employees at a particular job position.

(ii) Authority It means power to take decision. To carryon the responsibility every employee need to have some authority.

(iii) Accountability It means subordinates will be answerable for the non-completion of the task.

11. Decentralisation Decentralisation explains the manner in which decision making responsibilities are divided among hierarchical level.

12. Importance of Decentralisation

Develops initiative among subordinate

Develops managerial talent for the future

Quick decision making

Relief to top management

Facilitates growth

Better

6

---◦♭◦---

1. Staffing It consists of manpower planning, recruitment, selection, training, compensation. promotion and maintenance of managerial personnel.

According to Dale Yoder, "Staffing is that phase of the management which deals with the effective control and use of manpower or human resources."

2. Importance of Staffing

Filling the roles by obtaining competent personal

Placing right person at the right job

Growth of enterprise

Optimum utilisation of human resources

Helps in competing

Improves job satisfaction and morale of employees

Key to effectiveness of other functions

3. Staffing as Part of Human Resource Management When staffing function is carried on at a large scale, it becomes human resource management.

(i) Evaluation of HRM

4. Activities of Human Resource Management

Human resource planning

Recruitment, selection and placement

Career growth

Performance appraisal

Motivation

Compensation

Social security

5. Staffing Process The steps involved in the staffing process are

Estimating the manpower requirements

Recruitment

Selection

Placement and orientation

Training and development

Performance appraisal

Promotion and career planning

Compensation

6. Recruitment It refers to the process of appointing possible candidates for a job or a function. It has been defined as the process of searching for prospective employees and stimulating them to apply for jobs in an organisation.

7. Sources of Recruitment There are two sources of recruitment

Internal

External

8. Internal Sources Under internal source of recruitment the vacant job positions are filled by inducing the existing employees of the organisation

(i) Advantages

(a) It is economical.

(b) It motivates the existing employees. ,

(c) Through transfer employees get draining also in the form of job position.

(ii) Drawbacks

(a) No fresher new ideas will come in the organisation.

(b) There will be limited choice.

(c) Not suitable for new organisation.

(d) Frequent transfer may reduce the productivity of employee.

(iii) Methods Under the internal recruitment following methods of recruitment are used

(a) Transfer

(b) Promotion

9. External Sources When the candidates from outside the organisation are invited to fill the vacant job position then it is known as external recruitment.

(i) Advantages

(a) Fresh talent

(b) Wider choice

(c) Qualified personnel

(d) Latest technological knowledge

(e) Competitive spirit

(ii) Drawbacks

(a) The morale of existing employees goes down.

(b) Lengthy process.

(c) The new employees may not adjust in the rules and regulation of the organisation.

(d) It is expensive.

(iii) Methods

The common methods of external sources of recruitment are

(a) Direct recruitment

(b) Casual callers

(c) Advertisement

(d) Employment exchange

(e) Placement agencies and management consultants

(f) Campus recruitment

(g) Recommendations of employees

(h) Labour contractors

(i) Advertising on television

(j) Web publishing

(k) Factory gate

10. Selection It can be defined as discovering most promising and most suitable candidate to fill up the vacant job position in the organisation.

11. Process of Selection

(i) Preliminary screening

(ii) Selection test

(a) Intelligence test

(b) Aptitude test

(c) Personality test

(d) Trade test

(e) Interest test

(iii) Employment interview

(iv) Reference and background cheeks

(v) Selection decision

(vi) Medical examination

(vii) Job offer

(viii) Contract of employment

12. Training and Development

(i) Training raining means equipping the employeos with the required skill to perform the job.

(ii) Development It refers to overall growth of the employee. It focuses on personal growth and successful employees development.

13. Benefits of Training for Organisations

Reduced learning time

Better performance

Attitude formation

Aids in or help in solving operational problems

Managing manpower need

Helps to adopt changes

14. Benefits of Training for Employees

Better career options

Earning more

Boost up the morale

Less chance of accidents

15. Difference Between Training and Development

S.N.TrainingDevelopment

1It is process of increasing knowledge and skills.It is a processof learning and growth

2It is to enable the employee to do the job better.It is to enable the overall growth of the employees.

3It is a job oriented process.It is a career oriented process.

16. Training Methods

(i) On the Job Methods

(a) Apprenticeship programmes

(b) Coaching

(c) Internship training

(d) Job rotation

(ii) Off the Job Methods

(a) Classroom lectures

(b) Films

(c) Case study

(d) Computer modelling

(e) Vestibule training

(f) Programmed instruction

1. Directing Directing function of management is concerned with instructing, guiding, inspiring and motivating the employees in the organisation so that their efforts result in achievement of organisational goal.

According to Ernest Dale, "Directing is telling people what to do and seeing that they do it to the best of their ability."

2. Characteristics of Directing

It initiates action.

Continuing function.

It takes place at every level.

It flow from top to bottom.

It is performance oriented.

It is human element.

3. Importance of Directing

To initiate action

To integrate employees efforts

Means of motivation

Balance in the organisation

To facilitate change

4. Principles of Directing

Maximum individual contribution

Harmony of objectives

Unity of command

Appropriate technique

Managerial communication

Strategic use of informal organisation(vii) Effective leadership

Follow through

5. Elements of Staffing There are four main elements of directing

Supervision

Motivation

Leadership

Communication

6. Supervision The supervision means instructing, guiding, monitoring and observing the employees while they are performing jobs in the organisation.

(i) Role of Supervisor

(a) Role of mediator or linking pin

(b) Role of a guide

7. Importance of a Supervision

8. Motivation Motivation can be defined as stimulating, inspiring and inducing the employees to perform to their best capacity. Motivation is a psychological term which means it can not be forced on employees.

9. Interrelated Teams of Motivation

Motive

Motivation

Motivator

10. Characteristics of Motivation

Motivation is a psychological phenomenon.

Motivation produces goal directed behaviour.

Motivators can be positive as well as negative.

Motivation is a complex process.

Motivation is a dynamic and continuous process.

11. Process of Motivation

Unsatisfied need

Tension

Drive

Search behaviour

Satisfaction need

Reduction of tension

12. Importance of Motivation

Motivation helps change negative attitude to positive attitude.

Motivation improve performance level of employees.

Helps in achieving the organisational goal.

Motivation creates supportive work environment.

Motivation help the managers to introduce changes.

Reduction in employees turnover.

13. Need Hierarchy

Theory or Maslow's Need Hierarchy theory Need or the desire is a very important elements in motivation because the employees get motivated only for their needs.

Maslow has given a sequence or hierarchy of needs in the follows way

(i) Physiological needs

(ii) Safety and security needs

(iii) Social or belonging needs

(iv) Esteem needs

(v) Self-actualisation needs

14. Assumptions of Maslow's Need Hierarchy Theory

(i) Behaviour of people depends upon their need. Human behaviour can be changed or motivated by fulfilling their needs.

(ii) Generally the needs follow the hierarchy i.e ., starting from physiological need.15. Financial and Non-Financial Incentives Incentive means all measures which are used to motivate people to improve performance. These incentives may be broadly classified

(i) Financial Incentives The reward or incentive which can be calculated in terms of money is known as monetary incentive.

The common monetary incentives are

(a) Pay and allowances

(b) Profit sharing

(c) Co-Partnership/stock option

(d) Bonus

(e) Commission

(f) Suggestion system

(g) Productivity linked with wage incentives

(b) Retirement benefits

(i) Perks/Fringe benefits/perquisites

(ii) Non-Financial Incentives The incentives which can not be calculated in terms of money are known as non-financial incentives.

The common non-financial incentives are

(a) Status

(b) Organisational climate

(c) Career advancement

(d) Job enrichment

(e) Employees recognition

(f) Job security

(g) Employee's participation

(h) Autonomy/Employee empowerment

16. Leadership It is a process of influencing the behaviour of people at work towards the achievement of specified goal.

(i) Features of Leadership

(a) It indicates the ability of an individual to influence others.

(b) It tries to bring change in behaviour.

(c) It shows interpersonal relationship between leader and followers.

(d) It is to achieve common goal.

(e) It is a continuous process.17. Different Styles of Leadership

(i) Autocratic or Authoritative Leadership

17. Different Styles of Leadership

(i) Autocratic or Authoritative Leadership

(ii) Democratic or Participative Leadership

(iii) Free-rein or Laissez-Faire Leadership

18. Importance of Leadership

(i) Helps in inspiring and guiding the employees.

(ii) Secures co-operation of the members of organisation.

(iii) Creates confidence.

(iv) Improves productivity.

(v) Improves job satisfaction.

(vi) Improves team-spiritor group cohesion.

19. Qualities of a Good Leader

(i) Physical qualities

(ii) Knowledge, intelligence and scholarship

(iii) Integrity and honesty

(iv) Self confidence and sense of responsibility

(v) Initiative

(vi) Communication skill

(vii) Decisiveness

(viii) Social skill

20. Communication It can be defined as transmission or exchange of ideas, views message information or instruction between two or more persons by different means.

21. Communication Process

22. Importance of Communication

Act as basis of co-ordination and co-operation

Act as basis for decision making

Increase managerial efficiency

Establish effective leadership

Helps in process of motivation and morale development

Helps in smooth working of an enterprise

Promoter co-operation and peace

23. Form of Organisational Communication

(i)   Formal Communication It refers to official communication   taking place in the organisation. According to direction of flow, formal communication can be divided into four types

(a) Downward communication

(b) Upward communication

(c) Horizontal communication

(d) Diagonal communication

Common Networks of formal communication are

(a) Wheel pattern

(b) Chain pattern

(c) Circle pattern

(d) Channel or free flow pattern

(e) Inverted 'V'

(ii)   Informal Communication Informal   communication between different members of organisation who are not officially attached to each other is known as Informal communication.

Common networks of informal communication are

(a) Gossip

(b) Clusters

(c) Single strand

(d) probability

24. Methods of Communication

Oral communication

Written communication

25. Barriers to Effective Communication

(i) Semantic Barrier

(a) Badly expressed message

(b) Symbols with different meanings

(c) Faulty translation

(d) Unclarified assumption

(e) Technical jargon

(f) Body language

(ii) Psychological Barrier

(a) Premature evaluation

(b) Lack of attention

(c) Loss by poor retention

(d) Distrust

(iii) Organisational Barrier

(a) Organisational policy

(b) Rules and regulations

(c) Status difference

(d) Complex organisation

(iv) Personal Barriers

(a) Lack of confidence

(b) Lack of incentives

(c) Fear of authority

26. Improving Effective Communication

Clarify the idea

Consult others

Use of proper language

Proper feedback

Communication for present as well as for future

Follow up

Good listener

Open mind

Completeness of message

8

1. Controlling It can be defined as comparison of actual performance with the planned performance.

According to Ricky W Griffin. "Controlling function leads to goal achievement. an organisation without effective control is not likely to reach its goals."

2. Importance of Controlling

(i) Helps in achieving organisational goods

(ii) Judging accuracy of standards

(iii) Making efficient use of resources

(iv) Improving employee motivation

(v) Ensures order and discipline

(vi) Facilitate co-ordination in action

(vii) Controlling help in minimising the errors

3. Limitations of Controlling

(i) Difficulty in setting quantitative standards

(ii) No control on external factors

(iii) Resistance from employees

(iv) Costly affair

4. Relationship Between Planning and Controlling

(i) Planning interlinked and controlling activities. are interdependent and

(ii) Planning and controlling both are forward looking function.

5. Controlling Process

(i) Setting up of standards

(ii) Measuring of performance

(iii) Compare performance against standard

(iv) Analysing deviation

(a) Critical point control

(b) Management by exception

(v) Taking Corrective measure

6. Deviation It refers to difference between actual performance and standard performance.

7. Techniques of Managerial Control

There are two technique of managerial control

(i) Traditional techniques

(ii) Modern techniques

8. Traditional Techniques

(i) Personal observation

(ii) Statistical reports

(iii) Break-even analysis

(iv) Budgetary control

9. Modern Techniques

(i) Return on investment

(ii) Ratio Analysis

(a) Liquidity ratio

(b) Solvency ratio

(c) Profitability ratio

(d) Turnover ratio

(iii) Responsibility Accounting

(a) Cost or expenses centre

(b) Revenue centre

(c) Profit centre

(d) Investment centre

(iv) Management Audit

(v) Network Techniques (PERT and CPM)

9

1. Business Finance Money required for carrying out business activities is called Business Finance.

2. Financial Management It refers to efficient acquisition of finance, efficient utilisation of finance and efficient distributing and disposal of surplus for smooth working of company.

According to Howard and Upton, "Financial management involves the application of general management principles to a particular financial operation.

3. Role of Financial Management

Size and composition of fixed assets

Amount and composition of current assets

The amount of long term and short financing

Fixing debt equity ratio in capital

All items in Profit and Loss account

5. Objectives of Financial Management

6. Financial Decisions

The financial functions relate to three major decisions which very finance manager has to take

Investment decision

Financing decision

Dividend decision

7. Investment Decision (Capital Budgeting Decision)

This decision relates to careful selection of assets in which funds will be invested by the firms.

Factors affecting investment/capital budgeting decisions are

Cash flow of the project

Return on investment

Risk involved

Investment criteria

8. Financing Decision This relates to composition of various securities in the capital structure of the company. Mainly sources of finance can be divided into two categories

Owners fund

Borrowed fund

Factors affecting financing decisions are

Cost

Risk

Cash flow position

Control consideration

Floatation cost

Fixed operating cost

State of capital market

9. Dividend Decision This relates earned. The major alternatives are to distribution of to retain the earnings profit or to distribute to the shareholders.

Factors affecting dividend decisions are

Earning

Stability of earning

Cash flow position

Growth opportunities

Stability of dividend

Preference of shareholders

Taxation policy

Access to capital market consideration

Legal restrictions

Contractual constraints

Stock market reaction

10. Financial Planning It means deciding in advance how much to spend, on what to spend according to the funds at your disposal.

11. Objectives of Financial Planning

To ensure availability of funds whenever these are required.

To see that firm does not raise resources unnecessarily.

12. Importance of Financial Planning

It facilitates collection of optimum funds.

It helps in fixing the most appropriate capital structure.

Helps in investing finance in right projects.

Helps in operational activities.

Base for financial control.

Helps in proper utilisation of finance.

Helps in avoiding business shocks and surprises.

Link between investment and financing decisions.

Helps in co-ordination.

It links present with future.

13. Capital Structure Capital structure means the proportion of dept and equity used for financing the operations of business.

Capital Structure = (Debt/Equity)

14. Financial Leverage It refers to proportion of debt in the overall capital

Financial Leverage = (D/E)

Where, D = Debt, E = Equity

15. Factors Determining the Capital Structure

Cash flow position

Interest Coverage Ratio (lCR) = (EBIT/Interest)

Debt Service Coverage Ratio (DSCR)

Return on investment

Cost of debt

Tax rate

Cost of equity

Floatation cost

Risk consideration

Flexibility

Control

Regulatory framework

Stock market condition

Capital structure of other companies

16. Fixed Capital Fixed Capital involves allocation of firm's capital to long term assets or projects.

17. Importance or Scope of Capital Budgeting Decision

Long term growth

Large amount of funds involved

Risk involved

Irreversible decision

18. Factors Affecting Requirement of Fixed Capital

Nature of business

Scale of operation

Technique of production

Technology upgradation

Growth prospects

Diversification

Availability of finance and leasing facility

Level of collaboration/joint ventures

19. Working Capital Working Capital refers to excess of Current assets over Current liabilities.

There are two types of working capital

Gross working capital

Net working capital

20. Operating Cycle

21. Factors Affecting the Working Capital

Length of operating cycle

Nature of business

Scale of operation

Business cycle fluctuation

Seasonal factors

Credit allowed

Credit avail cycle

Technology and production

Operating efficiency

Availability of raw materials

Level of competition

Inflation

Growth prospects

10

1. Financial Market Financial market is a link between surplus and deficit units or in other words financial market brings together lenders and borrowers.

2. Functions of Financial Markets

(i) Mobilisation of savings and channelising them into most productive use

(ii) Facilitates price discovery

(iii) Provides liquidity to financial assets

(iv) Reduces the cost of transaction

3. Classification of Financial Market

There are two segment of financial market

(i) Money Market It is a market for short term funds meant for dealing in monetary assets whose period of maturity is less than one year.

(a) Features of Money Market

Market for short term

No fixed geographical location

Major institutions involved in money market are RBI Commercial Banks, LIC, GIC etc.

Common instruments of money market are call money, treasury bill, CP, CD, commercial bill etc.

(b) Instruments of Money Market

Call money

Treasury bills (T Bills)

Commercial bills · Commercial Paper (CP)

Certificate of Deposits (CD)

(iii) Capital Market It is a market for medium and long term funds. It includes all the organisations, institutions and instruments that provides long term and medium term funds.

According to VK Bhalla, "Capital market can be defined as the mechanism which channellises saving into investment or productive use. Capital market allocates the capital resources amongst alternative uses. It intermediates flow of savings of those who save a part of their income from those who want to invest it in productive assets"

(a) Features of Capital Market

Link between savers and investment opportunities

Deals in long term investment

Utilises intermediaries

Determinant of capital formation

Government rules and regulations

(b) Types of Capital Markets The main components of capital market are

· Primary Market (New Issue Market) In this market, securities are sold for the first time, i.e., new securities are issued from the company.

Methods of Floatation The securities may be issued in primary market by the following methods

Public issue though prospectus

Offer for sale

Private placement

Right issue (for existing companies)

e-IPOs

Secondary Market (Stock Exchange) The secondary market is the market for the sale and purchase of previously issued or second hand securities.

4. Stock Exchange It defines as "an organisation or body of individuals, whether incorporated or not established f01' the purpose of assisting. regulating and controlling of business in buying, selling and dealing in securities."

5. Types of Operators in Stock Exchange

Brokers

Jobbers

Bulls

Bears

Stag

6. Functions of Stock Exchange/Secondary Market

Economic barometer

Pricing of securities

Safety of transactions

Contributes to economic growth

Spreading of equity cult

Providing scope for speculation

Liquidity

Better allocation of capital

Promotes the habits of savings and investment

7. Trading Procedure on a Stock Exchange

b. Some Benefits of on Line Stock Exchange

Demutualisation

Dematerialisation

9. All India Level Stock Exchange India has two All India level stock exchanges. These are

National Stock Exchange of India (NSEI)

Over The Counter Exchange of India (OTCEI)

10. Common Features of NSEI and OTCEI

Nation wide coverage

Ringless

Screen based trading

Transparency

Incorporated entities backed by financial institutions

11. NSEI It was recognised in 1992 and started working in 1994.

It launched the capital market segment in November 1994 and option segment in June 2000 for various derivative instruments.

Objectives and Nature of NSEI are as follows

Securities traded – Capital market + Money market

Payment and delivery in 15 days time period

12. OTCEI The OTCEI was incorporated in 1990. The trading started in this exchange in 1992. This exchange is established on the lines of NASDAQ the OTC exchange in USA.

Objectives and Nature of OTCEI are as follows

Compulsory market makers to provide liquidity

Settlement period of OTCEI is one week

13. Securities Exchange Board of India (SEE!) It was set up in 1998 to regulate the functions of securities market. SEBI promotes orderly and healthy development in the stock market.

(i) Objectives of SEBI

(a) Protect the interest of investors.

(b) Promote and develop stock exchange dealings.

(c) Regulate the dealings.

(ii) Functions of SEBI

(a) Protective Functions

It checks price rigging.

It prohibits insider trading.

SEBI prohibits fraudulent and unfair trade practices.

(b) Developmental Functions

SEBI promotes training of intermediaries of the securities market.

SEBI has permitted .internet trading through registered stock brokers.

(c) Regulatory Functions

SEBI has framed rules and regulations and a code of conduct to regulate the intermediaries such as merchant bankers, brokers, underwriters etc.

SEBI registers and regulates the working of mutual funds etc.

SEBI regulate take over of the companies.

SEBI conducts enquiries and audit of stock exchanges.

11

---◦♭◦---

1. Market - It refers to the 'set of potential and actual buyers of a product or service'.

2. Customer - It refers to the people or organisations that seek satisfaction of their needs and wants.

3. Marketer or Seller The marketer can be a person or organisation who make available the products or services and offer them to the customer with an intention of satisfying the customer with an intention of satisfying the customer needs and wants.

4. Marketing It is a social process by which individuals and groups obtain what they need and want through creating. offering and freely exchanging products and services of value with others.

According to JF Pyle. "Marketing is that phase of business activity through which the human wants are satisfied by the exchange of goods and services."

5. Features of Marketing

Need and want

Creating a market offering

Customer value

Exchange Mechanism

6. Marketing Management It means management of all the activities related to marketing or in other words we can say. it refers to planning, organising, directing and controlling the activities which result in exchange of goods and services. Marketing management involves following activities

Choosing target market

Growing customers in target market

Creating superior value

7. Difference between Selling and Marketing The marketing and selling can be differentiated on the basis of

Scope

Objective

Focus

Start and end

Efforts

Supremacy

Approach

Demand

8. Marketing Management Philosophies

Production concept

Product concept

Selling concept

Marketing concept

Societal concept

9. Objectives of Marketing Management

Creation of demand

Market share

Goodwill

Profitable sales volume through customer satisfaction

10. Functions of Marketing

Gathering and analysing market information

Market planning

Product designing and development

Standardisation and grading

Packaging and Labelling

Branding

Customer support services

Pricing of products

Promotion and selling

Physical distribution

Transportation

Storage and warehousing

11. Role of Marketing

Role In firm

Role in the economy

12. Marketing Mix The marketing mix refers to the ingredients or the tools or the variable which the marketeer mixes in order to Interact with a particular market.

According to Philip Kotler, "Marketing mix are the set of marketing tools that firm uses to pursue Its marketing objectives in the target market."

Elements of Marketing Mix

Product

Place

Price

Promotion

14. Product The product element of the marketing mix signifies the tangible or intangible product offered to the customer which satisfies the need.

15. Classification of Product or Service Product or goods can be classified in two categories

Consumer goods

Industrial goods

16. Consumer Goods

(i) On the Basis of Durability

(a) Durable products

(b) Non-durable products

(c) Services

(ii) Classification Based on Consumers Buying Behaviour and Attitude

(a) Convenient goods

(b) Shopping goods

(c) Speciality goods

17. Industrial Product Industrial products are used as input or raw material to produce consumer goods, e.g., tools, machinery etc.

Features of industrial produced are

Number of buyer

Channel of distribution

Geographical concentration

Derived demand

Technical consideration

Reciprocal buying

Leasing

18. Types of Products Industrial goods are classified as

Material and parts

Capital item

and business services

19. Product Mix It refers to important decisions related to the product such as quality of product, design of product packing of product etc.

(i) Branding A brand is the identification of a product. It can be in the form of a name, symbol or design etc.

(ii) Various Terms Related to Brand

(a) Brand

(b) Brand name

(c) Brand mark

(d) Trade mark

(iii) Advantages of Brand Name

(a) Helps in product differentiation

(b) Helps in advertising

(c) Differential pricing

(d) Easy introduction of new product

(iv) Advantages to Customer

(a) Helps in identification of product

(b) Ensures quality

(c) Status symbol

20. Packaging It can be defined as a set of tasks or activities which are concerned with designing, production of an appropriate wrapper, container or bag for the product.

(i) Level of Packaging There are three levels of packaging

(a) Primary packaging

(b) Secondary packaging

(c) Transportation packaging

(ii) Importance of Packaging

(a) Rising standard of health and sanitation

(b) Self service outlets

(c) Product differentiation

(d) Innovational opportunities

(iii) Functions of Packaging

(a) Protection

(b) Identification

(c) Convenience

(d) Promotion

21, Labelling It means putting identification marks on the package

Functions of labels are as follows

Describe the product and specify its contents

Identify the product

Helps in grading

Promotes sale

Providing information required by law/legal requirement

22. Price Price is the value which a buyer passes on to the seller in lieu of the product or service provided.

23. Price Mix It refers to important decisions related to fixing the price of a commodity.

The factors kept in mind while fixing the price of a commodity or service

Pricing objectives

Product cost

Extent of competition in the market

Customer's demand and utility

Government and legal regulation

Marketing methods used

24, Pricing Strategies There are two pricing strategies

Price skimming

Penetration pricing

25. Place/Physical Distribution Place refers to the set of decisions that need to be taken in order to make the product available.

26. Place Mix It refers to important decisions related to physical distribution of goods and services. These decisions are deciding the channel of distribution, market for distribution.

27. Channels of Distribution

28. Functions of Distribution Channels

Sorting/Granding

Accumulation

Variety

Packaging

Promotion

Negotiation

Risk taking

29. Types of Distribution Levels

(i) Zero Level Channel/Direct Channel

(ii) Indirect Channel

30. Factors Determining Choice of a Channel

Product related factors

Competitive factors

Company related factors

Market related factors

Environmental factors

31. Components of Physical Distribution

32. Promotion Mix It refers to all the decisions related to promotion of sales of products and services.

Following are the tools or elements of promotion. They are also called elements of promotion mix.

Advertising

Sales promotion

Personal selling

Publicity

33. Advertising It can be defined as the paid form of non-personal presentation and promotion of ideas, good or services and by identified sponsor.

34. Advantages of Advertisement

Reach

Choice

Legitimacy

Expressiveness

Economy

Enhancing customer satisfaction

35. Disadvantages of Advertisement

Less forceful

Less effective

Difficulty in media choice

Inflexibility

Lack of feedback

36. Objections to Advertising

Adds to cost

Undermines social values

Confuses the buyers

Encourages sale of inferior products

Some advertisements are not appealing

37. Different Media Available for Advertising

Newspapers

Magazines

Television

Outdoor

Internet

38. Sales Promotion It refers to short term use of incentives or other promotional activities that stimulate the customer to buy the product.

39. Sales Promotion Techniques for Customers

Rebate

Discount

Refunds

Product combination

Quantity gift

Instant draws and assigned gift

Lucky draw

Usable benefit

Full finance @ 0%

Sampling

Contents

40. Merits of Sales Promotion

Attention attract

Useful in new product launch

Synergy in total promotion efforts

Aid to other promotion tools

41. Demerits of Sales Promotion

Reflect crisis

Spoil product image

42. Personal Selling Personal selling means selling personally.

This involves face-to-face interaction between seller and buyer for the purpose of sale.

43. Features of Personal Selling

(i) Personal interaction

Two-way communication

Better response

Relationship

Better convincing

44. Qualities of a Good Salesman

Physical qualities

Social qualities

Mental qualities

Other qualities

45. Publicity Publicity is a non-paid form of impersonal communication
(i) Merits of Publicity
(a) More credibility
(b) Mass research
(ii) Limitations of Publicity
(a) Firms have no control
(b) Limited information

12

1. Consumer A consumer is generally understood as a person who uses consumer goods or avails any service.

2. Consumer Protection It means protecting consumer from the clutches of fraud producers or sellers.

3. Who Can File a Complaint?

A consumer

Any registered consumer association

The Central Government or any State Government

One or more consumers, on behalf of numerous consumers having the interest

A legal heir or representative of a decreased consumer

4. Three Tier Judicial Machinery to Provide Protection to Consumers

- District forum
- State commission
- National commission

5. Consumer Rights

- Right to safety
- Right to be informed
- Right to choose
- Right to be heard
- Right to seek redressal
- Right to consumer education

6. Consumer Responsibilities

- Consumer must exercise his right

- Consumer must be conscious
- Filling complaints for the redressal of genuine
- Consumer must be quality cautious grievances
- Do not be carried away by advertisement
- Insist on cash memo

7. Ways and Means of Consumer Protections

- Self regulations by business
- Business association
- Consumer awareness
- Consumer organisation
- Government

8. Relief Available

- Removal of defects from the goods
- Replacement of the goods
- Refund of the price paid
- Compensation of loss or injury suffered
- Removal of deficiency in service
- Discontinuance of unfair trade practices
- Stopping the sale of hazardous goods
- Withdrawal of hazardous goods from market

9. Rule of Consumer Organisations In India, several consumer organisations and non-governmental organisations have been set up for the protection and promotion of consumers interest. These associations are performing following functions

- Bringing out brochures, journals etc
- Spreading consumer awareness
- Collecting data of different product
- Filing suits or complaints on behalf of customers
- Educating the consumer to help themselves
- Educating women regarding consumerism

10 Rule of Press A part from publishing articles, columns etc newspapers have tried to provide protection to harassed consumers by including a consumer complaint column.

11. Rule of Universities and Press IGNOU has made a beginning by developing a complete syllabus which provides a framework for the universities to develop a curriculum for consumer education CBSE has published a teacher's manual on consumer education.

13

1. Introduction Entrepreneurship is process of setting up one's own business. The person who sets up business is called on entrepreneurship.

2. Meaning Entrepreneurship is a systematic purpose full and creative activity of identifying a need, mobilising resources and organising production with a view to delivering value to the customers.

According to Peter Drucker, "Entrepreneur-one who is involved in gathering and using resources to opportunities to produce result."

3. Characteristics of Entrepreneurship

Systematic activity

Lawfull and purposefull activity

Creative activity

Organisation of production

Risk taking

4. Relationship between Entrepreneurship and Management

Entrepreneurship is concerned with starting of a new business venture, management assures efficiency and success of business starts by entrepreneur.

In developing countries, entrepreneurs remain attached to day-to-day activities also and managers also remain in touch with strategic divisions of entrepreneurs.

5. Functions of Entrepreneurs in Relation to Economic Development

Contribution to gross domestic product

Capital formation

Employment generation

Generation of business opportunities for others

Improves economic efficiency

Increasing the scope of economic activities

Growth of local communities

Boosting the spirit of exploration, experimentation and daring

6. Process of Setting Up a New Enterprise The steps involved in setting up of a business are

Scanning the environment

Development of product/service

Feasibility analysis

Appraisal by funding agencies (financial institution)

Resource mobilisation

Project commissioning and councling (establishing of an enterprise)

Adoption and management of growth

7. The Process of Entrepreneurship Development

Individual Personality of Entrepreneur It means competence, motivation, values and attitude of the entrepreneur.

Environment Factors It refers to economic Frame work. industrial and trade policy, institutional framework of our country.

8. Role of Environment in Entrepreneurship Development

Environment conditions have Entrepreneurship Development. Inflation good infrastructures entrepreneurship development.

9. The Role of Individuals in Entrepreneurship Development

Entrepreneurial competencies

Entrepreneurial motivation

Entrepreneurial values and attitudes

10. Entrepreneurial Competencies

Initiative

Recognising and grabbing the opportunities

Persistence

Collecting information

High quality work

Commitment

Efficiency

Planning

Problem solving

Self confidence

Assertiveness

Persuasion

Use of influence strategies

Monitoring

Concern for employees welfare

11. Entrepreneurial Motivation

Need for achievement
Need for power
Need for affiliation
Need for autonomy
12. Entrepreneurial Values
Theoretical doctrinal values
Social values
Aesthetic values
Political values
Economic values
Moral values